BEYOND NORMAL PRAYER
The Redemptive Power of Suffering

Ad Majorem Dei Gloriam

dedicated especially to
those who suffer from severe ME,
the people who care for them,
and all who fight for justice and truth.

GREG CROWHURST

Beyond Normal Prayer
The Redemptive Power of Suffering

Reflections on the Messages to the
Sick and the Suffering and
Salvifici Doloris of Pope John Paul II

ST PAULS

ST PAULS Publishing
187 Battersea Bridge Road, London SW11 3AS, UK
www.stpauls.ie

Copyright © ST PAULS 2006

ISBN 085439 717 5

Set by TuKan DTP, Stubbington, Fareham, UK
Printed in Malta by Progress Press Company Limited

ST PAULS is an activity of the priests and brothers
of the Society of St Paul who proclaim the Gospel
through the media of social communication

Contents

Foreword

In the past, I have avoided spiritual books dealing with the subject of suffering. Working closely with people who have physical, learning and complex disabilities and with their carers, I have shared a lot of pain. Who wants to read about suffering, when it is there in abundance, and so vividly portrayed? That was my excuse. Then, though frequently rubbing shoulders with chronic sorrow, rejections and powerlessness, I was not acquainted with persistent grief at a personal level. That was before; whereas now, as a reader of this book, I am no longer a bystander to suffering. Once a compassionate observer, I am now someone alert to any fruitful framework which might help illuminate my own watershed of prolonged anguish.

The author has offered such an insight. He, a long-term Christian carer; the person cared for, his wife Linda with an active prayer ministry. Greg Crowhurst speaks directly to those who live with prolonged suffering, without any platitudes, but from experience. He draws the reader by the powerful words of Pope John Paul II to the significance of weakness, speaking from the heart of his own suffering as he repeatedly did and drawing on the Pope's great Apostolic Letter *Salvifici Doloris* "On the Christian Meaning of Suffering".

I welcome this book for dipping into for some reflection to keep me going on dark days. At other times it will be, as when I first read it, similar in effect to a personal letter for me alone. Most helpful are the short poignant prayers at the end of each section, and the prayers of Linda Crowhurst in the Appendix.

This is a prayer guide, written eloquently from lived experience for others who live with suffering in its many forms.

Rosemary McCoskey, MBE

Prologue

Naked, that is how Christ hung on the Cross. Trying to hold on somehow, that is how Mary, his mother, stood with him at the foot of the Cross. Outside, on the edge, that is where the Cross stood.

Stripped of everything, that is how my wife has been for many years, every moment an unimaginable moment of agony. Day after day, year after year, being there, loving her, wanting God to take away the torment, that is how I have been. Outside, on the edge, existing on the borderlines, that is where we both are – sufferer and carer.

Such a powerful place, Calvary. That is the message of this book.

You have to be there to understand that the Cross and the Resurrection are one and the same. That is why Pope John Paul II was able to tower over the world stage and influence world history like no other modern world leader. Out of his sufferings shone the truth of the Cross.

A safe pathway through suffering, that is what this book offers to those in any kind of mental, emotional, physical or spiritual pain. For carers and sufferers it opens up a unique perspective, the Redemptive cycle:

Redemption is about transfiguration; be reborn.
Redemption is about potential; discover your
    personal power.
Redemption is about quest; open your eyes.
Redemption is about progress; grow.
Redemption is about transformation; change.

When intense physical, emotional, spiritual or mental suffering comes to you, you have a stark choice. Either you enter more deeply into the meaning of suffering, where you find Christ, not just as a theological idea or someone somewhere else, but living, alive with you, more deeply than you could ever have imagined before this suffering came upon you; or you choose a path of fear and despair.

This book opens up a pathway to help you more clearly see and understand the meaning and the possibilities open to you within your suffering. It is here that you come to meet the living Christ, all-merciful, all-loving, all-compassionate, all-embracing Christ, who knows every moment of agony and responds with love. This is the way you are led to know the greatness of God. This is the way to meet love with love and to find the true meaning of healing, not necessarily wellness.

Suffering sometimes is so great that the only way is through it, where there is no alternative other than to be in it. It is not the "why" of suffering, so much as the "how" of suffering that is illuminated here to deliver a path of hope.

Asking "why" can lead to helplessness and despair. Asking "how" can lead to hope and freedom.

The path of suffering, as a mystical union with Christ, through him, with the Father and the Holy Spirit, leads you on a profound journey where you discover that you too can be part of the Redemptive cycle of love, where you too can offer up your own torment for the healing of the world and even more profoundly than that, you can fully enter into the mystery of the Cross and even dare to offer your heart to the One who suffers for all.

Introduction

This book is the outcome of a journey into the mystery of the Cross, not as an abstract idea but as the very means of survival, over more than a decade of suffering, every moment of every day. Pope John Paul II always emphasised the prophetic role that the sick and the afflicted have to play in the Church. Ironically, it is unlikely that we would have come across his teachings at all, as a carer and sufferer, had I not stumbled across an old, tatty, incomplete copy of *Salvifici Doloris,* several years ago.

Outlined in that document is a blueprint for the very Church we are longing for – one that not only reaches out but actively wants to learn from the sick and disabled, except that Church is hard to find in reality.

Yet struggling alone day after agonising day, week after week, year after year; with a body too sore to even touch, with sickness, and everything: job, career, money, status, friends, holidays and treats stripped away, yet still trying to live our marriage, God still guided us every step of the way, by providing exceptionally wise and loving guides – just ordinary people, who over the years have come into our life and stayed and prayed and been there for us.

The book arises mainly, though, out of my wife's mysticism. She has forged a theology of suffering out of prayer, tears and fire. Research has shown that her condition, severe ME, is equivalent to that of an AIDS sufferer two months before death, and that only in terminally ill cancer and stroke patients is the sickness impact profile greater. It just goes on, without relent. Her eyes though sparkle with light and her whole self shines with joy. When she prays it is most powerful; her theology is strikingly in tune with Pope John Paul's, it is almost as if his writings exactly describe her most intimate experiences of suffering and grasping hold of God.

This is a passionate account of suffering as prayed and lived through from the inside, as is *Salvifici Doloris* itself, which could only have been written by someone who has been there too.

How odd to reflect on the difference: one work proceeding from one of the greatest, most famous figures in the Church, the other from one of its least, at least in worldly terms.

A Safe Passage through Suffering

All who suffer are held in the power and love of Christ that pours out from the Cross. That is the message of Pope John Paul II's great work on suffering, *Salvifici Doloris*. Christ on the Cross reaches out to you and everybody, to every single pain, on every single level and offers it love, healing, forgiveness, redemption.

He offers a safe passage back to the Father, for that is his mission; to redeem all and bring truth, love and mercy. Christ's love is available and ever present. It is never imposed, it is waiting to be received and accepted. Christ in his longing to love and heal you waits for you to seek him.

He longs for you to ask for his help, that you may find the truth of love, in the very depths of pain.

He longs to embrace you that you may be led to a wonderful encounter with the living God. It is through him that all healing is possible.

In encountering Christ you are given the strength and the courage to say "Yes". You are blessed in an outpouring of Spirit. You enter into the heart of love.

For some there may be a miraculous healing, a lifting of suffering. For others there may be a peace within the suffering. Christ blesses you and enables you to survive, cope with, have courage within the place where you are, no matter what you are going through.

Somehow the way is lighter. Somehow you are lifted up.

You come in your humanity, God lifts you up into his divinity, the outcome of which is an outpouring of love and an abundance of blessings, peace beyond all knowing, joy unfathomable, truth unchallengeable. Even in this terrible place. Especially here.

Dear Friends, you see how important you are! So as you suffer in union with Christ be united to him in prayer. Remember Job: after enduring terrible pain and affliction, he prayed for his friends and "the Lord accepted Job's prayer" (Job 42:9). You too can pray very effectively for your fellow men and women, for the Church and for the world.

John Paul II, A prayer service in St Joseph's Church in Baroko, during which the Holy Father met and blessed the sick and preached the homily, 18 January 1995.

Your trials are a call to be greater than you ever thought possible.

You are empowered to greatness through suffering.

Love blesses you and you are transformed into more and more perfect love.

You can be certain of one thing, meeting Christ in a place of great pain transforms your life and change will occur, whether it be:

- a change of attitude
- a softening of mind
- a change of heart
- a physical healing
- a release of emotion
- a spiritual enlightenment

Change will transform your very being as you approach and are healed by love.

Lifted into the heart of love through the power of the Cross and the mystery of suffering, you encounter the Great and Holy Trinity in a oneness beyond words.

You find the love of God, the Father, Son and Holy Spirit living within you and bear witness to this fact by the peace that endures, a peace not of the world that enables you to cope and find strength and to keep reaching out in service.

Your whole life is gradually transformed into an act of giving, an outpouring of spirit that embraces the whole world.

Even if you are sick, even though you feel small and inadequate, even if you are dying, you are wrapped up in the mystery of life offered by the Father, through the Son, in the power of the Holy Spirit – this service of suffering.

Unless he calls you and touches you and enriches you with the power of the Trinity, you could not enter more fully into this place of pain and triumph. As you grow in love, as you find healing inside, you are touched with tenderness and mercy for all humankind; for each suffering brother and sister.

Encounter with Christ opens your heart to compassion. This is the meaning of suffering.

If you can say yes to Christ and more than this, if you can say yes to suffering and offer it to him who loves, you must alleviate in some tiny way the burden of pain he carries.

You enter into his mission of love in some small way. Bound by love the sufferer is entwined in the great mystery of compassion for every hurting soul.

This is the greatest act of service that a human can offer.

Is it not you brothers and sisters, who indeed by your suffering share in the passion of the Saviour, and in a certain way do complete it?

The first Audience held by John Paul II, in the Sistine Chapel on Wednesday 18 October 1978.

Your pain mingles with the pain of the world. You feel every hurt, you feel every grief, you feel every cry of desolation and you, too, want to bring healing and love into that desperate place.

And by that very intention, you do. It is only when

Christ holds you and heals you that you are then able to have a greater vision of your own service in the world. This is a mysterious and mystical union which may be unseen by the eyes of the unaware and undervalued or unknown. Yet great are the gifts and the healings as a result of such tender service to humankind.

It can only be received through great pain and suffering.

It can only be found from the inside through deep connection and great need.

It is the most wondrous and profound act of love and brings peace, patience, hope, joy to the giver and a unity with the Trinity that is powerful, close by and active in the world despite the apparent signs of affliction.

Dying Christ embraced all and in this embrace so he was embraced by the Father. If you embrace all in your suffering you become part of his divine act of oneness. You embrace and are embraced by Christ who is embraced by the Father. The Holy Spirit is released and miracles happen.

The whole universe is embraced in an act of love, interconnected and interwoven in time and space and beyond, to eternity. It is the purest act of divine love and wisdom that reunites all in the power of the Spirit. Thus you can call on the Holy Spirit in your need and for the need of others, knowing that you will be held, and in that holding all things can be endured and all love is given back.

PRAYER

> Lord help us,
> Lord heal us,
> Lord show us
> how we can serve you,
> even on the path
> of unrelenting suffering.

The Prayer of the Suffering Person

When you are suffering, prayer can become a struggle as well as a need so great and vast that it would be unimaginable to exist without it. If you are experiencing longer term suffering, you will probably go through many different stages of prayerfulness until eventually you find that God is with you, whether you are in a state of conscious prayer or not, and you may find that prayer is not necessarily what you thought it was.

> *Dear brothers and sisters – who are sick and suffering… Do not stop to pray for the Church!*
>
> The message of John Paul II for the Third World Day of the Sick, 11 February 1995.

You move towards an encounter with God through seeking him and this means facing your weak and hurting self. Finding love, mercy, forgiveness in the void of yourself leads you to a profound place of healing from which you can step into the endless love of God and find new meaning in your life. It is from this place that you come to see and know the oneness of souls and the possibility of entering through prayer into the mystery of salvation, through the love of Christ that now resides with you. The healing moment comes when you can see beyond the need for wellness and enter into the life-giving love that supports and comforts all.

You see beyond your earthly limitations, to the awesome power of God working in you and you find that physical passivity does not equate with the spiritual power unleashed through the presence of the Holy Spirit. From this place you can reach out and know no boundaries of earthly scale. You can pray for a single person, a community or indeed the whole world and know with absolute certainty that the love and mercy you feel for them will in some way be an act of healing because you are part of the healing love that blesses the world through Jesus Christ, Our Lord and Saviour.

There are many different forms and ways of prayer open to the one who seeks God. Here are some of the ways open to the struggling soul.

We are blessed with many options of *formal prayer*. The Church offers specific prayers for specific occasions, for example the Divine Liturgy; the Divine Office; the Our Father, Hail Mary, Glory Be; each a powerful prayer in its own right. There are the prayers of the saints and many Novenas for those who require some external aid in prayer.

Prayerfulness is more than saying the words of a prayer, however, and to be too rigid in one's expectations of yourself or another may inhibit the true nature of prayerfulness. It is the reaching out towards God, the genuine desire to connect with and to find expression in and to experience God that is all-important, rather than any given format. One Hail Mary said with passion and truth mingled in every word is maybe more powerful than one thousand Hail Mary's said from habit and without awareness and intention. In fact, words are not necessarily essential at all in the true art of prayerfulness. To be immersed in God, this is our aim.

To feel the comfort and strength, to feel the power of the Holy Spirit, to hear God speak to you in silence, these are all the fruits of deep prayerfulness.

Don't be surprised as you seek God that you will find him ever-present, ever-loving, all-compassionate and tender, full of mercy and respect. For this is not a one-way conversation, and many are the fruits and blessings poured out upon those who earnestly cry out to God in their need and open their hearts to God.

Even if that cry is angry or fearful, do not be afraid, for God is with you and he understands and knows your deepest pain and your deepest hurt and responds freely with love, for he understands and accepts you just as you are. What is amazing is the availability of all three, the Father, Son and Holy Spirit to meet your need, to know and understand you and to hold you in the heart of their love.

We turn to Christ: he has borne every pain, every hurt on every level. But do not forget the Father who has loved and held him, comforted and strengthened him and knows all the hidden secrets of despair and unlove. Neither forget the Holy Spirit that comes not as we wish, not as we predict, not within our control, but all-powerful, all-majestic, all-wondrous and miraculous. Never forget the awesome nature of the Triune God. Even when we feel beyond his reach, we can know with all certainty that this cannot be so for he has loved us all in every moment and it is love that is triumphant in our broken world. And prayer is the way to find this truth.

There is the prayer of *silence and stillness*, the prayer of *singing and praise*, the prayer of *repetition,* such as the Jesus Prayer, the Rosary or any one of the Litanies.

There is *meditation, contemplation, prayer for healing,* Anointing of the Sick*, prayer for others, prayer for ourselves.* There is even the silent prayer of the heart which knows no words but cries out to God.

There are the Psalms.

The Devotions of the Saints, to the Sacred Heart, the Divine Mercy, are a few of the many ways that we can confidently seek God. Yet even when none of these are accessible to us, for reasons of severe impairment, emotional distress, the dark night of the soul, shame, guilt, anxiety, we can cling to the truth of the Cross and offer up a silent witness to the pain of the world in our own living, suffering bodies and align ourselves with the suffering heart of Jesus.

We can offer up our whole lives, every activity, every inability, every hurt, anger, need for consolation as an act of service to the living God and still find meaning and hope. This, then, is the ultimate way of prayerfulness, to live in the heart of love, offering all and living all in God.

Even if you are in agony, even if you are dying, still you can find his presence there silently, loving you and you can feel safe and held in the timelessness of an eternal moment of now.

You are held in the heart of love and can feel yourself expand beyond the limitations and boundaries of a suffering body. You are transfigured by the presence of God within you and shine a great light in the world. You need do nothing physically, yet still you can radiate great light in the world, and many blessings flow from your gift of service, your being one with God, even in a place of profound pain. Nothing is wasted here. Everything is love.

We can get stuck in this notion of wellness – it is living that is important, living in Christ.

PRAYER

Lord, help me to remember
that nothing is wasted,
that every moment of pain can be transfigured
and can bring healing.

A Theology of Suffering

In what way are the suffering so close to Christ, and how do they share in his sacrifice, and what difference does this make anyway?

That is what we are going to explore now, using excerpts from Pope John Paul II's great document on suffering, *Salvifici Doloris*, as our framework.

> *Dearest brothers and sisters who are being put to the test, generously offer your pain in communion with the suffering Christ and with Mary, his most tender Mother... We ask all of you that suffer to support us. We ask precisely you that are weak to become a source of strength for the Church and humanity. In the terrible combat between the forces of good and evil, of which our contemporary world offers us a spectacle, may your suffering in union with the Cross of Christ triumph.*

The message of John Paul II for the Fourth World Day of the Sick, 11 February 1996.

In 1998 Cardinal Joseph Ratzinger describing Pope John Paul II said: "The pain is written on his face. His figure is bent, and he needs to support himself on his pastoral staff. He leans on the cross, on the crucifix." John Paul II himself, drawing upon the words of St Paul on the Good Friday before his death, said in a handwritten note: "I offer up in my own flesh the sufferings that are lacking to the passion of Christ for the sake of the church, for the sake of the world."

At his Funeral Mass, Cardinal Ratzinger, the future Pope Benedict XVI, stated how John Paul II, "interpreted for us the Paschal Mystery as a mystery of divine mercy." In his last book, he wrote: The limit imposed upon evil "is ultimately divine mercy".

My wife's face lit up when I read those words to her, for she could clearly see what John Paul II meant. "Yes!" she exclaimed, and this is why: divine mercy is all love, all healing, all mercy, all purity, poured out for all time from the Cross. It is the Heart of God wide open, holding all, healing all, forgiving all, loving all, redeeming all, and all we have to do is say "Yes". Divine mercy is absolute grace opening a path for everybody, back to purity, back to love, no matter how lost they seem to be, all are welcome, all are embraced.

Mercy

Is the greatness of love revealed upon the Cross. Mercy is the absolute acceptance of all. Mercy is the blessing of love. Mercy is greater than evil. Mercy lies beyond forgiveness. Mercy is a gift unbidden, flowing from the unconditional heart of love, given freely and tenderly with compassion and understanding. Mercy is God and God is Mercy.

On the Cross and through the Cross, the heart of love triumphs, the will of God is complete, and that will is love and mercy which pours out for all time from that moment.

Those who suffer, are very close to God, because in their suffering they are especially close to his love and mercy. They are involved in it, they are wrapped up in it, they are a part of it; if they choose to seek God within it.

The Cross

The Cross is the healing moment of all time. It is the moment of absolute power, where love triumphs over evil and all is made well. It is the opening-up of the heart of love. It is the pathway to oneness. It is the way to life. It is the supreme moment of clarity, where heaven meets earth, where immanence and transcendence collide and love breaks through to touch all hearts. It is the defining moment of the universal Redemption of the world. The Cross needs to be seen as a multidimensional gateway reaching up to heaven, bringing heaven and earth together in a previously unknown way, releasing the power of the Holy Spirit into the life of every person.

God used Pope John Paul II so powerfully because the Pope accepted his suffering and constantly chose to actively seek God within it. He lived in Christ and Christ lived in him, making his life such a powerful witness to love.

The why of suffering is ultimately beyond our understanding. We can look and find partial answers through looking at consequences, responsibilities and actions, but this does not give a full picture and can only be fully answered by God himself. Suffering is in the world and yet, ultimately Love is greater still, and it is this love, given by God, that suffuses all suffering and brings healing and hope to those who are in need.

It is only when you look to the mystery of suffering that Christ's divine healing act of love makes sense – for all the unhealed hurt in the world is held in that moment on the Cross. Your own suffering only makes sense in that you can hold it in Christ's love as he holds you in his love. Christ's own suffering can only make sense when seen in its spiritual context – an act of love for love's sake – the Father holding the Son, the Son holding you, all united by the power of the love manifest in the Holy Spirit.

There is some greater mystery here unfolding that only God can know the totality of. You can only make sense of it when you look with the eyes of love at the very meaning of existence.

And see Love shining back at you.

However dark the path or however difficult the way, God's light will lead you and give you safe passage, for out of great suffering and the deepest pain comes the most amazing message of Redemption, and many are the spiritual blessings poured out upon the world, from those who have the courage to follow in trust and confidence in the Lord.

Redemption

Is the saving grace of God. Is the pathway to the Father. Is the reception of all mercy. Is the cleansing and healing of all souls. Is the spiritual joy of oneness. Is love unbound.

One of Pope John Paul II's final messages to the sick was: "God has not forgotten you. Christ suffers with you. And by offering up your sufferings, you can collaborate with him in the redemption of the world." (Thirteenth Annual World Day of the Sick on 11 February 2005) Redemption of the world was also the theme of *Salvifici Doloris*; Pope John Paul II's ground-breaking 1984 Apostolic Letter on the Christian meaning of suffering. To begin he quotes St Paul who wrote: *In my flesh I complete what is lacking in Christ's afflictions for the sake of his body, that is, the Church.*

The Holy Father shows how you can enter into the salvation of the world through your own suffering, in a unique and powerful way. You too can contribute, more than contribute, you can complete, in some mysterious way, what is lacking in Christ's afflictions to bring healing into the world.

You too can participate and bring meaning to your own life by using your suffering as a powerful act of unity with Christ. There is an incredible link between the suffering person and the suffering Body of Christ; you can serve in this way because you have already been healed and touched by Christ on the Cross.

This is the meaning of suffering reunited with love, triumphant in the wholeness of Christ's suffering, by the grace of God; and that is the message of *Salvifici Doloris*; an extraordinary journey into suffering.

PRAYER

Lord, however small, ill, distressed,
incapacitated, afraid, I may be,
help me find you
and in the power of that finding,
let love be released and triumph.

SECTION TWO

Excerpts from and Reflections on
Salvifici Doloris

What follows are particular excerpts from *Salvifici Doloris*, chosen to illuminate the path of suffering and the greater path of salvific redemption.

It is especially to the weakest, the sick, the poor, and the afflicted that we would like to open our hearts, in the initial moment of this pastoral ministry.

The first Audience held by John Paul II in the Sistine Chapel on Wednesday 18 October 1978.

Called in a Mysterious Way

> *Suffering seems to belong to man's transcendence: it is one of those points in which man is in a certain sense "destined" to go beyond himself, and he is called to this in a mysterious way.*

(Salvifici Doloris 2)

The calling of the human person to go beyond themself in the mystery of suffering, comes most certainly from God. The choice is ours to follow. Always it is the grace of God that leads us to God and suffering seems the simplest, purest and most absolute way of finding him. This necessarily demands that we find a way to transcend the depths of sorrow and grief, the torment and terror that suffuses suffering.

The very existence of suffering, which for the human person is reality, living as they do, in a world of chaos, in a fragile and human body, will inevitably lead to a point that they are destined to go beyond. In fact they find that they must go beyond themself, in some sense, in order to transcend the misery of suffering.

We must see that the only real choice we have then, when suffering is unbearable, is to go within and beyond, to break open a spiritual path, to find that there is something greater still in that moment, and that is Love.

This is the entry point into the mystery of Redemption. The seeking to go beyond and into the suffering leads us directly to Christ. Here we find forgiveness, mercy, love, compassion, peace and that grace which instantly transfigures us and sets us on a path of transformation, that becomes a lifetime journey to wholeness.

PRAYER

Lord, in your greatness
help us when we feel small and lost.
Guide us ever onwards
with your perfect light.

Through the Cross

The Redemption was accomplished through the Cross of Christ, that is, through his suffering.

(Salvifici Doloris 3)

The Redemption could only have happened because of the sacrifice of Jesus Christ, the Son of the Living God. It is only through him, through his suffering, that the path of Redemption is truly once and for all opened up for all time, for all people, in all places. This is an immense gift, only made possible by the Son of God whose Spirit, in union with the Trinity, can reach out beyond time and space and heal the void between man and God, where sin exists and evil manipulates.

It may be hard to accept unless seen with spiritual eyes, that suffering was the only way, yet it is the reality of Christ's nature, being both human and divine, that unites us once again with the Father who is complete love and total mercy. Only he could have made this choice. Only he could have walked this path, only he could have held this pain, only he could have taken on the suffering and sin of all and triumphed, because only he had the power of God with him in that way that was necessary for the saving of humankind.

Only he, as both man and God, encompassing both humanity and divinity, could attempt this supreme act of love, with humility. Only he could say "I am the Way, the Truth and the Life", and mean it; because this is the truth of his suffering that was opened up on the Cross.

He is the truth that we can hold on to. He is the way to perfect oneness, healing and forgiveness. He is the life that is the light of man. He calls us on and gives us the hope of the world.

PRAYER

> Let us ask with boldness
> for healing and help.
> Let us ask with confidence
> in the name of Jesus Christ.

Meeting Man on the Path

> *Born of the mystery of Redemption in the Cross of Christ, the Church has to try to meet man in a special way on the path of his suffering. In this meeting man "becomes the way for the Church", and this way is one of the most important ones.*
>
> (Salvifici Doloris 3)

Those who suffer, those who have chosen to walk intimately with the suffering Christ and thus enter into the mystery of Redemption, are given tremendous gifts of wisdom, prayer, insight, knowledge and love of Christ. They are given great compassion and they come to know the mercy of God so intimately that they can and must be pivotal in the life of the Church. In their closeness and walk with the suffering Christ they have much to offer, in fact, the whole array of the Gifts of the Spirit will be manifested in them.

The Church, to be fully alive in the Spirit, has an obligation to reach out and open itself to these Graces.

Those who suffer must not be ignored, for they bring the truth of Redemption, the love of the Trinity into our awareness. To ignore them is to ignore Christ and to not understand the meaning of the gift of suffering; it is to ignore the meaning of Love poured out upon the Cross.

It is in this meeting place of suffering that man and Christ become one most intimately. This connection is essential to the aliveness of the Church. It is how we can genuinely become disciples, because it is when we reach out and find Christ in all his suffering and glory that we begin to open our hearts truly to love – to be able to receive, know and give love.

Through this, compassion is born in us. Thus a Church connected to this awareness finds its true direction, living in compassion, filled with the power of the Holy Spirit, the Kingdom of God is then, assuredly, very near!

PRAYER

> Grant us wisdom
> to know what is right.
> Grant us peace
> to act in truth.

Greatness of Mystery

> *Human suffering evokes compassion; it also evokes respect, and in its own way it intimidates. For in suffering is contained the greatness of a specific mystery.*
>
> (Salvifici Doloris 4)

For many it is too frightening, too radical, too overwhelming to look into the heart of pain, so that even when you feel compassion, even when you feel respect for the person who is suffering, yet still you dare not go the whole way into the complete mystery of another's suffering because its power is so great. When fully comprehended it is almost too much to dare to look, to dare to open yourself to feel, to dare to hear the acuteness of the pain or grief. Even though you long to, desire to help, there are very few who do not feel intimidated by the vastness of the experience.

It is the truly gentle, the truly open, the truly fearless who might glimpse the possibility, who might see beyond the actual physical reality, who might dare to know the awesome wonder and truth there to be found in the depths of the suffering soul.

Christ alone walks into this mystical space with a totally open heart and is not overwhelmed but stays there and holds us there. Mary by her complete offering of self and uniting of hearts, the Immaculate and Sacred Hearts, is pierced and yet stays and finds the triumph with her Son and touches the power of the truth of this mystery. So you need to cling tightly to them and then dare to tread beyond and through the pain and find the magnificent gift of Love held there. So do you move beyond intimidation into the Heart of Mercy.

Do not, then, be afraid or filled with trepidation. Do not be surprised by the vast possibility hidden within such dreadful experience. Do not be surprised that you feel small and helpless in the face of so much suffering, but always remember that Christ is with you in his mercy and the power of God who is love is always available to help you in the face of this enormous mystery.

PRAYER

Have mercy on us
in our weakness,
that we will always find safe passage
back to strength once more.

The Width of Suffering

Man suffers in different ways, ways not always considered by medicine, not even in its most advanced specialisations. Suffering is something which is still wider than sickness, more complex and at the same time still more deeply rooted in humanity itself.

(Salvifici Doloris 5)

You might say in some sense that to be human is to suffer; in fact, this must be so. When you trace humanity back to Adam and Eve and the nature of the Fall, suffering is deeply human and is perhaps somehow something more than pain or sickness in or of itself. Some people can endure great levels of physical pain and still not suffer in that sense, whereas others may suffer torments beyond belief.

Suffering in itself seems on some level to come from an inability to cope with or accept that which is, in itself, in that moment. Christ, because he is human, is able to go into the extremes of physical torment and pain, yet still remain himself within it. He is able to take on and reach out to every moment of every pain of every person and touch it with love that flows from the heart of his being.

It is perhaps this ability to be in the moment of suffering, without suffering the loss of love, that is so powerful. Suffering then, has two doorways:

- the doorway to freedom, to love, to endurance,

or

- the doorway to despair.

This is the choice within that we must all make. Yet it is Christ who reaches out beyond humanity, who contains all suffering in the heart of love, who reaches beyond the moment of intolerability and offers hope and healing and renewal, who offers a way back to the Father, in a new relationship.

All humanity by their very nature can suffer, yet all suffering can lead to a path of redemption and healing, totally divine.

PRAYER

> Even when we cannot see any way forward
> help us not to despair
> but to trust in your unfailing love
> to deliver us.

Clarity on Evil

Thus the reality of suffering prompts the question about the essence of evil: what is evil? This question seems, in a certain sense, inseparable from the theme of suffering.

(Salvifici Doloris 7)

You must embrace the question, "What is evil and how does it impact upon suffering and life?" if you are to hope to walk a clear and safe path through suffering and illness. It is important to understand the nature and the boundary of evil and indeed love, so that it can clearly be seen for what it is, and no more than that.

It is very important to understand that sickness of itself is not evil. That suffering is of itself not evil either, though it may be caused by evil. Yet if you are unable to touch the suffering Christ you are in danger of losing the truth and being overwhelmed; you allow the evil in to manipulate and twist, to lose your way. It is important to see the power that evil can hold so that it does not triumph, for held in the love of Christ, Christ is greater than all evil and holds all suffering so that the choice may be seen more clearly. Love overcomes all suffering because Christ, who is love, with the Father and the Holy Spirit has triumphed over all suffering and brings a pathway of hope through all evil, if you can choose to follow him, to align yourself with him, throw yourself upon his love and mercy.

Evil cannot follow, though physical suffering and sickness may remain. All suffering can be taken up into the cycle of Redemption by choosing God, by choosing love, not fear, by choosing mercy and forgiveness rather than punishment or persecution, by choosing freedom over judgment, by choosing hope not despair – and all because of love shining brightly upon the Cross.

PRAYER

> Free us from the fears
> that bind us and keep us
> away from truth
> and knowing you, Lord.

The World of Suffering

The world of suffering possesses as it were its own solidarity. People who suffer become similar to one another through the analogy of their situation, the trial of their destiny, or through their need for understanding and care, and perhaps above all through the persistent question of the meaning of suffering.

(Salvifici Doloris 8)

When suffering comes upon you and is vast and wide, it is sometimes possible only for those who are in a similar situation to really comprehend the immensity of your experience. The compassion that comes from sharing the same form of suffering leads to a profound solidarity, unshakeable from the outside and unique in its wisdom. As you reach out in your need, you may find the secret of pain: that hidden within the depths of incredible suffering there is another who suffers with you, most intimately and infinitely – one who knows every dimension of pain and suffering, and that is Jesus Christ himself.

He has already reached out in his own terror and torment and embraced you with his ever-loving, ever open heart. If you probe deeply into the meaning of suffering, you will find that there is always hope, for the One who loves all has offered his heart to you for all time and has triumphed over suffering by the power of love. His, then, is the greatest solidarity of all, for he knows suffering well and so is undeterred from the path. He is a shining beacon of Hope and his love knows no end. Thus you will find that he is always the one who remains with you in the closest solidarity and supplies your every answer.

Because your need is absolute, your reliance on God is total. You can triumph because Christ who has suffered all, holds all and is the path of healing for all. Christ brings transformation, illumination, insight, wisdom, comfort, strength, and a greatness that goes beyond suffering and leads to more than survival. He leads to the fulfilment of hope and even brings you to the possibility of joy and an inner peace most definitely not of the world.

Christ offers the greatest solidarity of all because he has held us all in our suffering and shared it and offered his own suffering as the greater path of love, which brings us into communion at a deeper level and shows us a new meaning of solidarity not present before Christ's death, resurrection and fullness of life.

Those who find God are able to find the hope and the truth of the resurrection and the miracle of sharing that true solidarity offers. They can then offer this awareness and solidarity to others like them.

PRAYER
Lord, help us to use our own
suffering to reach out to others in need,
help us to keep growing and saving the world in
our own special way.

Divine Love

> *Christ causes us to enter into the mystery and to discover the "why" of suffering, as far as we are capable of grasping the sublimity of divine love.*
>
> (Salvifici Doloris 13)

The "why" of suffering is embraced in the sublimity of divine love.

You cannot understand the "why" of suffering without the love of God. They are inseparable: no other way makes any sense. Without God's love embracing each suffering person, through Christ's own suffering on the Cross, all you have left is despair and death. But Christ has come to bring life, and he does this through the mystery of the Cross, the profound mystery of suffering held in love.

It is his energy holding you, it is his grace that touches you and empowers you to find strength greater than is possible, to find life when life seems impossible, to hold onto hope when despair is imminent and blesses you vastly with whole new vistas of awareness beyond the immediacy and desperation of your suffering, moment by moment. He leads you on and shines so brightly, that even in the darkness he can be seen and felt.

Reflecting on the "why" of suffering leads you to ask not only "why" but "how"; how can you continue to suffer in this place ? The answer here, too, is love.

PRAYER

>May we always find love as an answer
>to every problem, every pain,
>every feeling of hopelessness.
>May we find you, Lord.

Filling the Spiritual Space

In his suffering, sins are cancelled out precisely because he alone as the only-begotten Son could take them upon himself, accept them with that love for the Father which overcomes the evil of every sin; in a certain sense he annihilates this evil in the spiritual space of the relationship between God and humanity, and fills this space with good.

(Salvifici Doloris 17)

Jesus Christ goes into death and unites everything in the greatness of love. Therefore there is always hope of healing because there is always access to that love in every moment of existence. If you look upon sin as an absence of God or goodness, as a lapse from love, then you can begin to see how in Christ's suffering sins are cancelled out: because Christ in his absolute love, compassion and mercy completely united and always one with the Father, is able to enter into every infinite space, every breath, every heartbeat and every second between heartbeats even, and there place a seed, give nourishment and tenderly touch with love every weakness, every hurt, every fear, every anguish. Only he, through his divinity and his unity in the Trinity, can do this, can give this precious gift, because he holds humanity and divinity together through his holy sacrifice and infinite suffering, he is joined together to earth and heaven.

As he hangs upon the Cross, his arms stretched open, his heart is a pulse of love, of life, of healing, because he reaches out beyond the now in time and space to the infinite moment, to the end of time and beyond and holds all, receives all. He brings hope for all time. Evil has no power over him because the choice is his. He enters freely, with love at the centre and offers all, even his death, as a perfect sacrifice of love, that love might triumph.

Fear has already been triumphed over in the garden of Gethsemane and thus he enters into the passion of his Crucifixion in a triumph of power. Evil can do its worst but God's power is greater and evil is undone. The pathway to healing and hope and life is made open to all. Christ has extended into every aspect of humanity with tenderness and caring and shown himself to be greater, bound by the love of the Father and the Holy Spirit. He needs to enter into the depths so that life can be triumphant. He needs to experience even this so that all who die can be held in love and offered freedom of spirit.

It is this apparent emptiness of death, this void, which his spirit fills, that enables the triumph of love over evil and goodness to permeate. He is the alpha and the omega and as such unites all time and space in the mystery of Redemption. This all comes together by his absolute offering upon the Cross; it is the only way to complete the salvific cycle.

PRAYER

> However desperate or desolate
> we may feel, Lord,
> may we be restored
> by your love.

The Living Water of Life

> *The Cross of Christ has become a source from which flow rivers of living water.*
>
> (Salvifici Doloris 18)

It is only through this complete offering of life, where life triumphs fully, through entering into the furthest space away from God and returning in splendour, that the Holy Spirit can move freely in the world. The living water is ascribed to the Holy Spirit and thus the living water is seen to flow freely from the Heart of Love. Where Christ's side is pierced the water flows out and bears witness to Christ. This is further symbolised in the depiction of the Divine Mercy: through entering into death Christ's Spirit is freed to heal the whole world; all can now drink of the living water of life, for he brings life and new life and new understanding of life, carrying all with him and thus lifting us into the union of oneness, the utter place of healing, hope and joy, gifted by the Father, through the gifting of the Son.

Anyone now in time and space can step into the living water, be cleansed, be healed, be refreshed and strengthened, no matter how vast their suffering. No matter how far away they feel from God, through Christ's Passion we are all given a new gift of life in the Spirit. We can all be touched in any moment. We can all drink fully and be redeemed and saved. We can all triumph in Christ.

Through drinking the living water the miraculous becomes not only possible but imminent, and not only imminent but real. Not only real but true. And not only true but here. This, then, is the power of the gift of love and true fulfilment in Christ's earthly mission – his giving us the living water of life through the coming of the Holy Spirit.

<small>PRAYER</small>

> Thank you for the gifts of the Holy Spirit:
> gifts of healing and hope
> gifts of trust and prayer
> gifts of miracles and joy.

Sharing with Christ

If one becomes a sharer in the sufferings of Christ, this happens because Christ has opened his suffering to man, because he himself in his redemptive suffering has become, in a certain sense, a sharer in all human sufferings.

(Salvifici Doloris 20)

It is this mystery of humanity and divinity which Christ offers, which unites and unifies us all. It is through entering into the deepest, darkest places of pain and suffering, of loss and grief and touching all in love with his intimate and personal experience, that he feels our suffering. We in turn can feel his and therefore as he triumphs in love so we can also share in the Redemptive cycle, because each drop of pain he experienced was united with every single moment of every single person's suffering, for all people for all time.

Not only did he feel the absolute suffering of all humanity, he reached out further still and surrounded it with love. Therefore if you can find love in your own suffering, you can unite your own pain directly to his. Even such a gift as a whole lifetime of suffering, offered fully and freely by one human being will still only amount to a fraction of a second of Christ's burden of suffering on the Cross.

Yet, still, if you offer your own suffering to Christ in love, you become not a burden but a redemptive offering in solidarity with him. It is this love ultimately given by all of us that has already helped him to triumph.

As his suffering touches each of us, so our suffering, touching him, becomes a path which allows us to break through to union. Your love can therefore be used by Christ if you offer up your pain directly to him and this can then be used by him to ease in some true sense the pain of the world.

PRAYER

> May we accept every pain with humility.
> May we offer it up in love and service
> for the healing of the world.

Movement and Stillness

> *Those who share in Christ's sufferings have before their eyes the Paschal Mystery of the Cross and Resurrection, in which Christ descends, in a first phase, to the ultimate limits of human weakness and impotence: indeed, he dies nailed to the Cross. But if at the same time in this weakness there is accomplished his lifting up, confirmed by the power of the Resurrection, then this means that the weaknesses of all human sufferings are capable of being infused with the same power of God manifested in Christ's Cross.*
>
> (Salvifici Doloris 23)

As you experience the pain of your suffering and enter more deeply into this mystery it is important to remember that the Cross and the Resurrection are inseparable. It is possible otherwise to get lost in the immensity of suffering and lose the vision of hope that Christ brings us. It is essential to hold on to Christ as 'God-with-us' in the midst of all pain and suffering in order to see beyond, to glimpse the possibility of resurrection and all it means.

Yes, Christ dies on the cross and as such takes on our human frailty, but death is not triumphant: Life comes with the Power of Resurrection because Christ brings his divinity as well as his humanity to that infinite moment and thus we are all changed through the power of this truth. We can all, then, take part in the mystery of suffering, for human suffering is now infused with the power of love.

To lose sight of this unity may lead to a place

where pain seems endless and despair can follow. Or alternatively, to a place where you try to live in the spiritual world in an attempt to deny you bodily reality. In both these ways the truth of suffering and the gift hidden within are lost. Both are places of pain and helplessness if you remain stuck in them.

Approaching the Cross and embracing it can lead to a surprising new freedom. It is however, a process and a journey that must be worked through, especially for one going through intense suffering of mind, body, emotion, spirit. This is the path of movement and stillness, of feeling lost and stuck, yet with God's grace breaking through the barrier and finding the light shining brightly, illuminating the path ahead so that transformation is possible, and available by the love and grace of God.

This is the natural spiritual journey, incorporating the dark night of the soul with the infinite joy of transfiguration. You edge forward moment by moment as if on the edge of a cliff. Yet if you are able to take a step forward in faith, you will find the arms of love waiting for you. For Christ stands uplifted before you, shining his light as the lamp on the lamp stand. You will discover many blessings and gifts because you will find out the truth: that the path ahead always lies open to love.

PRAYER

> You give us the precious gift of life, Lord.
> May we grow to understand the wonder
> of this gift day by day.

The Redemptive Mystery

> *In so far as man becomes a sharer in Christ's sufferings – in any part of the world and at any time in history – to that extent he in his own way completes the suffering through which Christ accomplished the Redemption of the world.*
>
> (Salvifici Doloris 24)

If you choose to offer up your suffering, your pain, your grief, in whatever form it takes, and align yourself with the heart of love, the all-embracing Holy Trinity, you become wrapped up in the redemptive mystery offered by Christ, because you are no longer a burden of pain to Christ – you are sharing, through your own small act of love in bringing comfort and strength at the moment of the Passion to him. Your unconditional offering of your own suffering becomes part of the healing energy, part of the love that heals.

Christ's suffering upon the cross, his death and resurrection held by the Father and empowered by the Holy Spirit reaches out to the vastness of eternity. The power released therein reaches out across time and space and embraces every moment of existence and all within. This is how Christ is the alpha and the omega. This is how all is held and given safe passage back to the Father who is love and mercy. This is how all healing happens. This is the path, this is the way. This is why you can give no greater gift than to offer your own suffering in service and love to Christ.

This is how, by the mystical bond between us, we complete the suffering through which Redemption is achieved.

PRAYER

Lord, let every pain we suffer
be an act of love for you
to help in some small way
in the redemption of the world.

Spiritual Greatness

> *When this body is gravely ill, totally incapacitated, and the person is almost incapable of living and acting, all the more do interior maturity and spiritual greatness become evident, constituting a touching lesson to those who are healthy and normal.*
>
> *This interior maturity and spiritual greatness in suffering are certainly the result of a particular conversion and cooperation with the grace of the Crucified Redeemer.*
>
> (Salvifici Doloris 26)

Interior maturity and spiritual greatness can only be achieved through the grace of Christ crucified because it is only in the immediacy of extreme suffering that a path of healing can open up. As the physical body becomes more chaotic and unable to live in the world, so the spiritual world by God's grace can open up huge vistas of possibilities, immense blessings and give access to an immediacy of love not previously known or even sought, unimaginable without the breaking-open of illness.

The person blessed by the light of love shines a great light in the world. The visibility of Christ's indwelling becomes clear in the grace with which they overcome the immensity of their suffering. They then become a beacon of love, a light for those who are healthy and normal, especially if they can look with spiritual eyes upon the miracle of transformation presented to them.

It is here that the light of Christ shines most brightly, the light that can be seen so clearly if looked for with spiritual vision. Christ now so close, comes to live in that person and is truly known, seen and loved. His love and blessings in turn are radiated through the windows of the soul: the light of Christ can often be seen shining out through the eyes of ones who truly suffer and yet still triumph, for they are the ones who truly know compassion and mercy. They have been transfigured by Christ himself and have come to know him. Their hearts burn with passion and that passion is recognised in their radiance of light.

They triumph because Christ is with them: they no longer feel alone. The light of Christ is a beacon for the whole world. They have found a spiritual truth and freedom that touches all who see and know them.

The more hidden, ill and incapacitated, the closer they are to the truth of the love given out by Christ, even unto death. They are the ones with an incredible gift to offer: the gift of themselves in their suffering. This gift can then be used fully by Christ as part of the mystery of Redemption and healing of the world.

PRAYER

Lord, lead us on with your shining light,
so that when we can find no clear direction in
the world,
we can look to you with all certainty
and know the way to go.

Consoling Spirit

It is he himself who acts at the heart of human sufferings through his Spirit of truth, through the consoling Spirit. It is he who transforms, in a certain sense, the very substance of the spiritual life, indicating for the person who suffers a place close to himself. It is he – as the interior Master and Guide – who reveals to the suffering brother and sister this wonderful interchange, situated at the very heart of the mystery of the Redemption.

(Salvifici Doloris 26)

Because Christ died on the cross and gave out every drop of love, to embrace every one of us in our need, that love poured out returned in splendour of life in the Resurrection; through his Ascension into Heaven, the Holy Spirit was released in a new way into the whole world. Christ's redeeming love opened up a new path for us to find healing, hope, light, truth, meaning. He took all pain and sin onto himself and into himself and held it in the power of his love so that all experience of suffering might be used as journey to the Father.

Because of this all-encompassing, totally unconditional love that touches all of us, no matter how far away from God you may be or seem to be, there is promise of hope, there is a path back to truth, there is the possibility at every turn of finding love and transforming your life into goodness.

Christ's act of compassion, so immense it is almost unfathomable, can only come about through the action of the Spirit, which works in hidden and unseen places and spaces. It is an energy that you can come to feel and to trust and know and be consoled by, because it is so alive and truly present to you. Because of this massive release of the power of the Holy Spirit at Pentecost, this new way of receiving and knowing and coming to God is enabled.

So vast is the power and the possibility that no wonder miracles occur when you feel and touch and receive the Spirit of Love truly into yourself and when you offer it to others through your prayer relationship with the Trinity. Thus Christ can become your internal master and guide because he, through your openness and desire to know him, through grace, comes to live in you, as he promised. Thus you can hear him speak, you can become a channel of his healing graces, you can speak with authority because he is in you.

Christ's intimate relationship and oneness with the Father is offered to you, and through the power of the Spirit it is made possible. The interchange between man and God can frequently and more easily occur through the power of the Trinity working in oneness, if only you choose to open your heart to love and say "yes" to his Way.

PRAYER

> Lord, let us find hope always
> in the mighty Trinity
> especially when
> we feel helpless in ourselves.

Follow Me

> *Christ does not explain in the abstract the reasons for suffering, but before all else he says: "Follow me!". Come! Take part through your suffering in this work of saving the world, a salvation achieved through my suffering! Through my Cross. Gradually, as the individual takes up his cross, spiritually uniting himself to the Cross of Christ, the salvific meaning of suffering is revealed before him. He does not discover this meaning at his own human level, but at the level of the suffering of Christ.*
>
> (Salvifici Doloris 26)

It is only by entering into suffering and experiencing it first hand that you can truly come to grasp Christ's meaning and his love for you. It is the acceptance and the living through of such suffering that leads you more deeply into a spiritual journey, for this is where you meet Christ and where your way becomes united with his Way.

Christ on the cross immerses himself utterly and completely in his suffering, making it an act of total acceptance of all suffering for all time for all people. This is an immense and unfathomable gift of self-sacrifice. It is in this place that he holds you. It is in this place that you meet him. This is how you too can enter into a path of healing and love, for it is in this meeting point of suffering that you can be united with Christ himself and thus the power of the Trinity is released in your life and all who you hold within it.

This is the place where his words, "Follow me" take on real authenticity and new meaning. They come alive with possibility, for he calls you not to suffer but to be transfigured in your suffering. He calls you to transformation, the transformation of your own small fragment of suffering into something greater, that unites with him in bringing salvation to the whole world.

A clear pathway then opens up for you, if you accept his call to follow. You actively take part with him in saving the world, by using your suffering and embracing Christ in his suffering, because Christ holds all that suffering in a most powerful heart of love.

When Christ says "Follow me", he means follow me into the light, follow me into the truth, follow me into the mercy that can be found here. He means feel and know the truth – a truth that if I were to just tell you about it, you might not believe it possible. In truth, picking up your cross is actually the way to love unconditionally and in finding the gift, in giving unconditionally, you discover something even more amazing: love returns to you in even greater abundance than the love you are able to give, because it is united in spirit with Christ's love which is endless and boundless and empowered by the Holy Spirit and inspired by the Father who is absolute love.

PRAYER

> We may not always understand your
> way, O Lord,
> yet we ask for wisdom always
> to see your hand at work in all things.

A New Motherhood

> *As though by a continuation of that motherhood which by the power of the Holy Spirit had given him life, the dying Christ conferred upon the ever Virgin Mary a new kind of motherhood – spiritual and universal – towards all human beings, so that every individual, during the pilgrimage of faith, might remain, together with her, closely united to him unto the Cross, and so that every form of suffering, given fresh life by the power of this Cross, should become no longer the weakness of man but the power of God.*
>
> (Salvifici Doloris 26)

It is only through great suffering that great compassion can truly grow. Thus the heart of man, so intimately linked by a bond of love beyond words, is intricately linked with the Spirit of God and the redemption of the world. Such an ultimate gift of acceptance, freely chosen by Mary at the Annunciation and continually reaffirmed throughout her life with her Son, can only be rewarded.

It is such an immense gift that Mary offers by saying "yes" and continuing to say "yes" through every loss and change, through every pain experienced and felt throughout her life, that there must inevitably be a linking of immense spiritual benefit to the whole world and a spiritual reward or blessing for Mary as a result. Her role is so unique, so open-hearted, so perfectly trusting and so faithful that the compassion she must gain from this service, that she alone can offer to God, is profound. In his absolute tenderness towards her, he reaches out towards her upon the Cross and does not leave her alone in isolation, but tenderly provides for her earthly life by the gifting of John to be her son. More than this, there is a far deeper spiritual meaning for Mary is to be the mother of the whole Church, is to continue in a new role of motherhood. This is the spiritual gift.

The spiritual realm is broken open and the power of love pours forth from the heart of Christ and floods through the heart of Mary, widening her compassion and service for the whole world, beyond the actual time of her life on earth. It is only through this unique relationship between Mother and Son, their hearts linked forever, that this new level of healing and hope and transformation is released and made possible.

Mary's spirit is thus transformed in a perfect act of love for her Son and guarantees a pathway for souls to find that tenderness and comfort that can only be given by one who knows the deepest pain. This is the breaking open of the heart held in the power of the Holy Spirit, which finds even greater love and generosity at the centre, where perhaps one would imagine only a void might be left.

Love triumphant on the Cross, in the deepest, darkest place, is reflected in the prayers of Mary, who acts as a perfect example for us all in her triumph over evil, by trusting in God.

PRAYER

> We thank you for the Mother of God,
> whose gentle love blesses our lives,
> and in whose prayers
> we have total confidence.

A Special Grace

Down through the centuries and generations it has been seen that in suffering there is concealed a particular power that draws a person interiorly close to Christ, a special grace.

(Salvifici Doloris 26)

If you dare to enter into the place of pain and go more deeply into the suffering there present, you will find, surprisingly, that God too is present, not just as an idea or a concept, but as love, present, tender, true, and truly with you.

An amazing thing then occurs: the power of the Spirit is released in your life, whether it is to help you cope with insufferable pain beyond normal endurance, or to offer you a new vision of hope. The power of love working in your life is vast and many-faceted and is a God-given grace.

You come to see, feel, know Christ himself in his own suffering and you find that your own heart is broken open with tender compassion for him and all those he serves.

This, then, is how he draws you interiorly close. There is no boundary separating love from love. As love touches your broken heart, so love is born anew and Christ can use you most powerfully and intimately as a source of goodness, kindness, compassion and healing for others. Those who are called in this way have an opportunity to give a unique and precious service to the Son of God, and through him, to others.

The grace of God given to you enables you to draw even closer to the Son, and through this you can feel his presence. It is this awareness of Christ that enables you to go forward in love and it is indeed a very special grace. You are no longer alone. You are empowered and blessed, and the blessing of God draws you ever closer still and calls you to a path of transformation and hope not previously seen.

PRAYER

Help us Lord, to use our own suffering
to reach out to others in need.
Help us to keep growing and serving the world in
our own special way.

Joy

A source of joy is found in the overcoming of the sense of the uselessness of suffering, a feeling that is sometimes very strongly rooted in human suffering. This feeling not only consumes the person interiorly but seems to make him a burden to others. The person feels condemned to receive help and assistance from others and at the same time seems useless to himself. The discovery of the salvific meaning of suffering in union with Christ transforms this depressing feeling.

(Salvifici Doloris 27)

Evil would rejoice in the sense of uselessness that pervades all suffering and attacks our very senses. So much is given up when you are placed in a situation of great suffering, especially if that suffering is linked to physical illness. If you only look on suffering with the eyes of the world, then evil might triumph. But when you look with spiritual grace upon your earthly situation a new pathway is opened up: the path to healing, the pathway to love.

Feeling completely dependent on another can at first feel upsetting, disappointing, humiliating even, until you discover that your dependence really is upon the Son of God, who meets you both in your physical experience of suffering, through the love and care of others and internally through his direct spiritual presence. His light transfigures you so that you can see the truth of your situation. Dependence itself is then transformed into an act of humility and tenderness. Everything, then, can be transformed through a life lived in Christ and offered to him for the healing of the world. Your tiny life as seen from the outside becomes a life of immense vision and possibility when viewed with the eyes of love and united with Christ who suffers with you.

A source of joy is then unleashed as you see that you are not helpless or hopeless. The power of love is held within you and you can be part of a far greater mystery – the mystery of salvation no less! What joy indeed.

PRAYER

> May hope burn ever brighter
> in our hearts,
> and joy of knowing you
> fill our lives Lord.

The Power of Redemption

> *It is suffering, more than anything else, which clears the way for the grace which transforms human souls. Suffering, more than anything else makes present in the history of humanity the powers of the Redemption.*
>
> (Salvifici Doloris 27)

It is only when you truly suffer, when you find yourself in hopeless places; it is only when you, overwhelmed by the fear, pain, grief, unimaginable torment that constitutes true suffering, find yourself clinging to the only One who can be truly with you, the only One who knows you fully because he has opened his heart totally to each one of us in the intimacy of his space of suffering; it is only then that you find the truth of love. And this truth is most definitely and absolutely a grace from God.

It is only when you have no place to hide, have no place to go, have no choice but to let go of your immediate experience, that you know true poverty of spirit. It is only in that instant of knowing that you find the ever-present brilliant God here-with-us; that transformation opens up new meaning and becomes an absolute reality. To experience such moments and to find that beyond despair love lies waiting, is truly miraculous. It is only really from this place that knowledge is born and redemption becomes a tangible reality which you experience and share.

It is only you who have been in that place, which may take many forms, who can say, with certainty and wisdom, that you know that Christ is with you. It is the surest path to truth and to light. It is not a path that you would choose from an earthly perspective but from a spiritual perspective once it has been experienced, true freedom is known and love can pour into compassion for the whole world.

PRAYER

> We are called to love you.
> Let us come, then,
> in all humility
> and serve you, Lord.

A Good Samaritan

> *Everyone who stops beside the suffering of another person, whatever form it may take, is a Good Samaritan. This stopping does not mean curiosity but availability.*
>
> (Salvifici Doloris 28)

Everyone has goodness at the heart of their being, gifted by God. It is this source of goodness that you must seek to find, no matter how hidden you may feel it is, no matter how battered you are by the world. This is the call of the Good Samaritan: to find that goodness and to reach out in love across barriers of hatred, difference, disease, even death.

Whenever the suffering of another calls on your door, or comes down your way, there is an opportunity to be a Good Samaritan. To look with eyes of love and kindness on your brother or sister, to see beyond the immediate situation, to reach the heart of need.

If you are called by Christ, if he lives in you, if you have chosen to love him, then you can begin to see the truth of oneness in the need of others and you can stop to help with an open heart. It is this openness of heart that says I am available to you, I am available for you, I can see your wounds and I want to love you.

This too, then, becomes part of the redemptive cycle of love and embraces Christ's Passion.

This is the blessing of love given to those who see the pain of the path ahead, yet choose to stay. This is the blessing of Mary, the mother of God, of Mary Magdalene and of John the Evangelist, for they are the ones who stayed and stood by Christ in his Passion.

They are the ones who looked with eyes of love on the saviour of the world, the beloved Son, teacher, friend: they are the ones who stayed and reached out despite their aching hearts. They are the ones who prayed despite the feeling that all was lost. They are the ones who despite fear, stood there for love.

It is when you come to this place at the foot of the cross and choose to remain for love, that love brings healing, and comfort, and that love can then be shared with the whole world.

This, then, is what is meant by availability to another: to stand with and by them, to watch with grief and pain yet still to trust, to pray, to hope, still to tenderly care: to "be" love to the very end and beyond.

This is what it means to be a true Samaritan – this is the path the Cross opens up for us. This is the way of love.

PRAYER

Reach out your healing hand, Lord.
In every situation that we find ourselves
may you show us how you can save.

Called Personally

The eloquence of the parable of the Good Samaritan, and of the whole Gospel, is especially this: every individual must feel as if called personally to bear witness to love in suffering.

(Salvifici Doloris 29)

Through living in the world, which is potentially a place of chaos on every level, it is inevitable that you will be touched by suffering and know the suffering of others. By aligning your whole life to Christ in his goodness, you are called personally to bear witness to love in suffering; the emphasis being on love.

Through Christ's love, you come to know in your own suffering that his love is with you, in you and it is greater than any suffering you are asked to bear. Through Christ living in you, you find your heart softening and melting. You find that he is lighting a passionate flame that burns in the centre and enables you to go out with the tenderness of the Father and offer your love to others.

Every time you reach out, beyond your human abilities, God's love flows with you and empowers you to amazing acts of self-sacrifice and tenderness, beyond the imaginable, because you are all held in the mercy of God and blessed and strengthened in every step of your journey. You can offer yourself in service then and bring the gift of hope to the hopeless, the gift of love to the fearful, the gift of life to the depressed.

Love shines in your heart and it is that love which bears witness.

It is as though everyone who acts as a Good

Samaritan stands at the foot of the Cross and though you may weep and though you may fear, love conquers all; love triumphs and heals. Love asks you to bear witness through your own personal call.

PRAYER

> Lord, help me to praise when I feel unable.
> Help me to pray when I feel helpless.
> Help me to trust that you will help.

Paradox of Passivity

> *The Gospel is the negation of passivity in the face of suffering.*
>
> (Salvifici Doloris 29)

Everything that you can see or know or discover in the Gospels leads you always towards the Passion, leads you into greater understanding and knowledge of the truth of Christ. This, however, is not always apparent, and your reading needs to be done in company with the Holy Spirit, so that you can discover the many different layers of truth available in the Word of God.

The Passion itself is in some sense a paradox. Christ comes into the world to turn everything on its head, to shake everything up, so that you can see things in new ways; new things are possible absolutely because of Christ's presence. The paradox is the seeming passivity and helplessness of Christ when viewed with earthly eyes versus the absolute power of a life given totally and utterly in service for the healing and loving of all people, for all time, in all places, both before and after the hours occupied by the actual Passion. This is the power of the spiritual realm.

This is the power of choice made in purity and obedience for the totality of reconciliation, for the undoing of evil. This is the choice where heaven and earth meet, where humanity and divinity expand into the infinite, bringing love and mercy into every moment of space and existence. There is nothing passive about the offering of life, previously unavailable in this way.

There is nothing passive about entering into the utter pain and misery, the desolation and desperation created by sin and evil – and being greater than it.

The Gospels can never be seen as passive because he enters where everyone has feared to go, even to death and hell, and he returns a triumphant victor; bringing hope unimagined and unimaginable.

PRAYER

Lord, when the troubles of the world seem
overwhelming,
and when fear grasps hold of our minds,
help us remember the truth of your promise
that you are with us always.

A Source of Strength

We ask precisely you who are weak to become a source of strength for the Church and humanity. In the terrible battle between the forces of good and evil, revealed to our eyes by our modern world, may your suffering in union with the Cross of Christ be victorious!

(Salvifici Doloris 31)

It is precisely those who are weak or who feel weak, who know that their strength comes from Christ, for they need to cling tightly to him. It is only those who suffer, who know such poverty of spirit, who learn to rely completely and utterly on Christ, who come to know the suffering Christ, who can identify and feel the love that dwells in the darkest places.

It is only when you have cried out in your utter weakness and helplessness and discovered that Christ is there – and more than that, that he knows and loves you in the intimacy of this impoverishment – that you can become a source of strength for the Church and all humanity.

Even though you may be bed-bound, housebound, totally physically disabled, paralysed – emotionally or physically – it is from this place that the truth of love shines bright and can radiate out in unimaginable, unforeseen ways to touch the hurting world. This is how love triumphs, because it goes beyond adversity and shines a light on truth.

The Holy Spirit flows in all moments, through all of time and can carry us with him, to embrace every hurting soul, no matter how physically far away. There is no distance between souls, held in the heart of love, transported by the Spirit, held in the heart of all mercy and compassion, united with the Father by the one supreme act of complete abandonment of self, offered by the Son to triumph over evil once and for all time.

It is the power of Christ's offering, even to death, that opens a pathway to complete Redemption which you can enter into at any moment of life you choose.

Those who suffer greatly see the choice more clearly and can say, "Here is my heart too. Let me embrace all in unity with Christ my Saviour. All glory is given to God who triumphs forever. Amen."

PRAYER

When doubts and fears set in to undermine
our faith, Lord,
help us to be strong, remembering you are love.
And nothing is greater than this truth.

The Redemptive Cycle

Drawing together the reflections on *Salvifici Doloris,* we illustrate the process of growth through suffering using the Redemptive Cycle.

THE REDEMPTIVE CYCLE
OFFERED FROM
THE CROSS

Experiencing
Suffering

Having greater
compassion for
yourself and others

Seeking God
within the
suffering

Finding new
freedom

ENCOUNTER

Living in
the Spirit

Finding Christ
in the centre
with you

Your life being
transformed

Receiving the
gifts of
the Spirit

Receiving forgiveness,
mercy, love,
tenderness,
compassion

Being transfigured by Christ's gift of
light / life / love

Pain that will not go away

What do you do with physical, mental, emotional or spiritual pain that does not go away; with pain from which you cannot escape? Often the only way through pain, of coping with pain, is to find some way of simply being within it. From the point of view of our existence in time and space the only way is to go through it, because time and space are linear and you have to find some way, some element of deep inner peace or space that belongs to you. You have to find some space that is not damaged by the experience, and from a spiritual point of view, you want to transcend the moment.

That transcendent spiritual energy connects you with the place you need to seek, for that place of being that is beyond the moment yet holds the moment, is something greater than the experience. That energy is Christ. So connection with the source of all goodness, all love, all compassion, all tenderness, all healing, lifts you or enlightens you or brings you to a deeper place of knowing in your being, a place that is blessed and loved. The energy of Christ holds all in that perfect moment of love, which he suffered and endured on the Cross. Since he gave that we are able to receive and find the deepest place of acceptance and goodness that cannot be obliterated, because we become united with him and he is triumphant.

Because we live in time and space, we are going to be battered by events, by pain; we are going to be physically, mentally, spiritually attacked and wounded because of the nature of being human. We are not always going to be able to stay in that transcendent space. But we can find a path that will lead us always back to that place, where Love is. Christ was battered, he was tormented and treated with total injustice. He was exposed to absolute evil, yet because he was one with the Father and the Spirit, it sustained him through, as he now sustains us. And it is because of his humanity, which is uniquely linked with his divinity, that we are able to enter into experiencing his love and be lifted to touch the transcendent and go beyond to a place of healing love. Despite any worldly experience, all is held in the power of God, who is love, and thus love can enter in through that sacrifice and gift that is all.

You have to:

- Place the situation in prayer
- Enter into the pain
- Find the freedom that goes beyond any central experience, because it is the freedom of love.

It does not mean it will not hurt, it does not mean you do not feel helpless. It means you will find a place that is not damaged by outer experiences, the true self, the heart of yourself, linked to the heart of love, the Trinity, that cannot be obliterated by evil because Christ has triumphed, no matter how bad it may seem. There is always a spark of light, and that light is the light of men and it cannot be extinguished.

You that bear the weight of suffering occupy the first places among those whom God loves... Manage to be generous witnesses to this privileged love through the gift of your suffering, which can do so much for the salvation of the human race.

The message of John Paul II for the Fifth World Day of the Sick, 11 February 1997.

As you grow you enter more fully into truth, and that is healing. You are standing up for truth and fighting back against evil and even if you are crucified, if you stay in the truth, you unleash the power of light and love on the world that cannot be extinguished because you have the whole power of heaven within you. You give out love and love returns in splendour, even more abundant than you gave, because it is unstoppable.

So you can never be helpless or hopeless, even if you feel it, because help is always there and hope is always there and it is all-enduring and never-ending. Even if it sometimes feels hidden, that is an illusion that comes from untruth. The power of love is an unstoppable power and blesses all truth and will not be hidden.

This process is not necessarily straight; you are probably going to keep going round the redemptive cycle (please see the diagram: The Redemptive cycle offered from the Cross) as you enter more deeply into Christ and cope with your suffering. However, once you have touched and felt the love, the light, the truth, the intimacy of the experience with Christ, of suffering, something new is born in you that can begin to grow, for you are not alone, however deep your pain and however entrenched your situation. You have the power of the Trinity working with you and in you, and this brings a different energy to help you live your experience more fully. It brings a mystical aspect whereby you can grow in love and be in service to the whole world through that mystical union, even if and especially if, that physical, mental, emotional and spiritual suffering is not alleviated.

Once you have connected with the living presence of God, the power of the Spirit can be alive and active within you, and the full gifts of the Spirit will become manifest and radiant in your life, as you offer your whole experience as an act of love and mercy to others, united forever in the healing love of Christ. Your life will be transformed, either immediately through a miracle or gradually; for most of us it is a process of learning to live and grow in Christ, of giving up our ego and learning humility, of learning how to love. That love is threefold:

- You have to learn to love yourself.
- You have to learn how to enter into a loving relationship with Christ.
- Only then can you truly enter into a relationship with and love everyone else: family, friends, neighbours, even enemies.

The transformation is a lifelong journey, which enables you to find new freedom: of forgiveness, of spirit, of expression, to see with new eyes and clarity, with wisdom, discernment and knowledge.

As you enter more fully into knowing and serving God, you do not do it alone. You have the most compassionate heart of the living Christ within you. The heart of love, the Father, Son and Holy Spirit is united with your heart, so that all healing, all compassion, all love, lies open for you to be part of, to experience, to know and to give.

It may be that for some people, healing of their situation comes, that their circumstances change, that their sickness leaves them, but the cycle of redemption is offered from the Cross and it is the Cross, when seen in all truth that is the most powerful place to find love.

Those of you who cannot escape from their suffering, therefore, have the closest relationship to the One who is love and the most powerful act of service can be given by you.

Entering into the Redemptive Cycle

To cope with suffering, to find something beyond it, you have to look. There are three levels, yet all are linked:

- Self
- God
- Other

You need to begin to love yourself, if you are going to cope with suffering. You need to seek your true self when you are suffering, because it is your true self that needs healing. You need to look within.

If you are not aware of yourself, how can you find God? You have to be ready to find God. Maybe seeking God also means seeking yourself. Ask yourself: are you seeking God, are you relating to God within this situation?

Where in Christ's life, Passion, Resurrection, could you sense Christ experiencing your pain?

Where is his suffering linked to yours?

To relate to Christ's suffering is a step to healing, because you are stepping outside yourself. By touching his pain you establish a link. He is reaching out to you, but you are also reaching out to him. You surely cannot feel that there is no one else now, that you are lost and alone still.

You might need to challenge your image of Christ. Is it true? You may need to find him in a real way, not a theological or a fictional way.

How do you find the real Christ? It is the living presence of the living God who suffers with you. When you find Christ beneath the layers that need working through, it feels good and liberating. When you seek him through the layers you find him in the centre with you.

Reaching out to him in his pain is a moment of compassion that lifts you outside of your own suffering into something greater, which is love and mercy, tenderness and compassion. These are his gifts to you.

You feel mercy, love and tenderness for him in his pain and he feels it for you, and there is a blessing of giving and receiving as they are born in your heart. When that happens, it is a moment of transfiguration. You are transfigured in that moment. You are no longer a lost soul; you are true self. The illusion is banished.

If you can meet Christ in that place, then you can see the truth, and that gives you strength and new vision and a new way of dealing and coping with the suffering. You are given a spiritual strength and healing happens.

This is a moment of illumination, of transfiguration. As a result of experiencing a moment of trust, of truth, of contact with Christ, you are in a different place – but in what way?

When you meet Christ you receive mercy, love, forgiveness and compassion. The process of transformation that happens through experiencing the Holy Spirit, living in the Spirit, receiving the gifts and fruits of the Spirit, helps you to find a new freedom in your life.

We are not saying your external situation is necessarily going to change. It is a freedom within, a much more compassionate understanding of yourself. You will struggle because you are still experiencing the suffering. The external suffering may not change, but you can change how you feel within it.

Transfiguration is a moment of freedom.

Transfiguration is living that freedom in your whole being, and it leads to a process of transformation because you will become aware of the different, unhealed parts of you that refuse to be silenced and need to be touched by that light and be united with Christ. The key is Christ: encountering Christ and continuing to encounter Christ in each part of yourself that is not healed so that gradually you develop greater awareness of your whole self and you find healing for your whole self.

The way is Christ, and it will take a whole lifetime. It is entering into Christ, finding compassion for yourself; and unless you find it, you cannot have compassion for others. The more you seek, the more you find.

So you enter back into the cycle, with the unhealed parts that come up; those parts of you that have not yet found freedom, that need to seek and encounter God in order to heal.

> *Dear people who are ill, a special place is reserved for you in the Church community. The condition of suffering in which you live and the wish to recover health make you particularly sensitive to the value of hope. To the intercession of Mary I entrust your aspiration to bodily and spiritual wellbeing, and I exhort you to enlighten and elevate it with the theological virtue of hope, a gift of Christ.*
>
> The message of John Paul II for the Sixth World Day of the Sick, 11 February 1998.

What you have as a result is an ongoing sense of growth, struggle, reaching in and reaching out. The more you experience inner healing, the more you can bring healing outside you. Whether your circumstances change or not, you grow spiritually, mentally, emotionally, and all things are possible. Your pain can be used because it is suffused with love. And love is triumphant even over death, as Christ shows us.

Close your eyes and seek God within. Wait until you see, feel, know, become aware of the truth of him within you. Feel his light, his love, his truth radiating out, touching every cell within you, every part of you blessed by goodness, touched by love bringing healing and hope. Seek and you will find the truth of God within you, the truth of love in you, the truth the light of life brings. Find the gifts waiting to be used. Nurture the seeds of goodness, of love, of creativity, of joy, and ask God to help them grow in you that you can use them and give the gift given to you to help the world outside. Every time you feel lonely, low, desperate, hurting, lost, remember to seek for Christ who lives within you and knows all, heals all, loves all – and find restoration of peace and the hope to go forward into light.

A Carer's Perspective:
Standing at the Foot of the Cross

The carer carries the person suffering in their heart to the foot of the Cross and there, in their pain, grief and their own helplessness, they stand alongside Mary and the others who were present at the crucifixion (John 19:25).

The author once recorded:

> So many tears, tears from deep within, tears of sadness, of frustration, of anger, of loss, of rage. Holding her close through the pain, anxiety and irritation. Holding her with all the strength I can muster, as best I can. Just her and me. Day by day. Hours on end. Holding when I can, which isn't always.

We stand with Mary at the foot of the Cross. Sometimes it is terrible and incomprehensible being a carer. Sometimes it is agony. Sometimes all we can do is stand there. You need to enter fully into the heart of Redemption to use every aspect of love and pain carried within you. Nothing is wasted. All is transformed into love.

> *I wish to encourage all who dedicate themselves zealously to caring for the sick to continue in their precious mission of love and find in it the inner consolation which the Lord grants to those who become Good Samaritans for their suffering neighbour.*
>
> Pope John Paul II's Address for the Ninth World Day of the Sick, 11 February 2001.

Suffering has this ability to bring you to the end of your own resources, so that you are better able to encounter God: "Pay attention, come to me; listen, and your soul will live" (Is 55:3).

To give and give, to discover one's poverty of mind, spirit, body and emotion can bring you, as a carer, to the point of despair. How often do we sink into guilt when we inevitably fail as a carer? How harsh are we upon ourselves? Yet it is mainly in these moments, when we are brought up short, when we are afraid or bewildered or disorientated, that we turn to God with a frequently uncomprehending cry for help. The bubble of our self-esteem has been pricked, our complacency has gone, and we are totally vulnerable.

We do not always realise how much God is with us. We are tempted to believe that the trials we endure come from God rather than God is with us in all our trials and will never let us down; when we face ourselves, our situation, our fear.

When we turn to God we find peace, not through trying, but in letting go of trying. His light shines upon and illuminates the truth in a moment of transfiguration. And that truth, no matter how painful it might seem, will always be wrapped in gentleness, compassion, caring, mercy, healing and forgiveness. Transfiguration is the entry point through suffering; it is the point of incredible power, it is a point of freedom.

We bring all of our self to the foot of the Cross. God meets us in the midst of our experience and struggles. We come to him as we are, so he can hold us in our pain. So he can care for us.

Find a still centre and be with God. Place everything in his hands. Be still. There you will feel his care, his strength, his touch. And give all to him, who has already touched every pain.

At the foot of the Cross we enter into partnership:

- with Mary in all our helplessness;
- with Jesus on the Cross, sharing in his pain, as he shares in ours;
- with the risen Christ, reaching out to the world, completing his mission of Redemption;
- with the apostles at Pentecost, receiving and living in the Holy Spirit.

We bring our total selves to the foot of the Cross:

MIND	BODY
EMOTION	SPIRIT

and through the redemptive power of the Cross we find that all things are possible after all; that our:

- awareness can be lifted from thoughts of limitation to love, compassion and healing;
- our pain can be transformed into a gift to be used;
- our feelings of isolation, distress and grief can be converted into feelings of oneness, joy and wholeness;
- our spiritual emptiness, our feelings of torment and spiritual attack can be transfigured into rebirth, restoration, triumph and glory.

You will learn the truth
and the truth will make you free.

John 8:32

Transfiguration

Is an illumination of truth where the inner light is revealed, where the light shines through in a whole and complete way. It is a glimpse of your true essence, it is a vision of what is perfect, whole and complete in you, of what God made you to be. When we are transfigured Christ's light shines in us because he lives in us and he illuminates the goodness in us and enables a new vision of life to proceed. For we can then carry that light in our minds and hearts and nothing is the same again.

Transformation

Is a process enacted through time and space. When love touches it transforms, changes and brings new direction and growth. Although transformation becomes possible immediately, there are many levels of living out this transformation. There are many parts of us that need healing and changing. So although it can be immediate, it is often a gradual process that evolves.

God has given you gifts and talents to use. Some you will discover very powerfully through caring, as you learn to serve and continue to serve. His power working in you frees you to love.

Caring for someone is a challenge that brings so much pain, but potentially so much reward! In any situation you do not have to be stuck – in fear, isolation, grief, bereavement, addiction, pain. It is amazing what is on offer to you, through the power of the Trinity. It is precisely in this struggle that we discover the great gift of unconditional love, to the extent that we sincerely give of our self to the other.

In the giving of our self, we find our true self; and our limitations and our wounds, our struggles as a carer, are a gift, because they lead us to God.

The quest, then, hidden within the path of caring for another, is to discover your mission, the true purpose and meaning of your life. This may not be what the world would necessarily value or see with the same eyes. Our situation as a carer takes on new hue, a different light, when looked upon with the eyes of love. Christ's mission was the greatest mission of all, an act of pure love offered to all for all time. His was the greatest expression of love; he loves each of us just as we are, in all our struggles and pain.

As you see yourself and your situation in a more understanding, less judgmental, more aware, more compassionate way, you begin to grow. Caring is a powerful call to love, to progress in the Spirit, to open your hearts to new meaning. You are called to be greater than you ever thought possible, you are empowered to greatness through suffering for love. Love blesses you and you are transformed into more and more perfect love:

> You did not choose me,
> no, I chose you;
> and I commissioned you to go out and bear fruit.
>
> John 15:16

Both carer and sufferer are transformed on this path; both are challenged and are asked to grow and serve in their own way in love. There is no greater task than to love in this way.

> This is my commandment:
> love one another as I have loved you.
>
> John 15:12

As we meet Christ in his suffering, he meets us in ours. This is the narrow road. It requires us to walk a straight path. We encounter not only Christ but we are lifted into the heart of love; the Great and Holy Trinity.

Many are the gifts and great is the love poured out; love that heals the world.

PRAYER

Lord, as I stand at the foot of the Cross,
with my heart breaking,
feeling too afraid to carry on,
feeling overloaded and dismayed,
help me to find the truth of love within,
that goes beyond all suffering and lifts us all into
the heart of love.

SECTION THREE
Enwrapped by Love

Truly, there is no better summing up of the message of *Salvifici Doloris* than the life of Pope John Paul II which we now investigate; such a witness to the extraordinary power of suffering and love.

> *Soon after my election to the Chair of St Peter, I came to "Gemelli" General Hospital and said that in my papal ministry I will very much need the support of those who are suffering... Today I reaffirm this conviction... I invite all the sick to join me in offering their pains to Christ, for the good of the Church and all humanity.*

The Marian Prayer of Pope John Paul II, transmitted on the radio direct from Gemelli, Rome, 24 May 1981.

A Life of Suffering

"Do not worry about this illness or about any other misfortune. Am I, your Mother, not here at your side? Are you not protected by my shadow? Am I not your safety?" The humble Indian, Juan Diego of Cuautilan, heard these words on the lips of the Blessed Virgin in December 1531, at the foot of Tepeyac Hill, today called Guadaloupe, after asking for the healing of a relative.

The message of John Paul II for the Fourth World Day of the Sick 1996.

In 1929, when he was only nine he lost his mother whom he had only ever known as ill. He underwent a strict but kindly upbringing by his impoverished, conservative father. He later wrote: "I had not yet reached the age of my first communion when I lost my mother, and she thus was unable to experience the joy of seeing that day, a day she had looked forward to as a great joy."[1] Very soon after his mother's death he lost his young sister too.

Three years later, his eldest brother Edmund, a doctor, died of scarlet fever, an event that had a deep impact upon him: "My brother Edmund died from a virulent epidemic of scarlet fever in the hospital where he was embarking on his medical career. If it had happened today, antibiotics would have saved him. I was twelve years old. The death of my mother left a deep mark on my memory, but perhaps that of my brother left an even deeper mark because of the dramatic circumstances in which it took place and because I was older."[2]

His father, a retired army sergeant, died in 1941. However, this death taught him that "a fully human and conscious serene death does not cause fear but renders the life of those who are present at this death more serious and encourages them to engage in deeper reflection."[3]

As a boy he swam in the flooded Skawa River, and in the winter the future pontiff played ice hockey on the Skawa's frozen surface and went skiing.

The young Karol Wojtyla was a talented athlete, a drama student, a singer song writer and a gifted actor who later went on to found the Rhapsody Theatre in Krakow. He was also a very keen sportsman.

He variously worked as a messenger for a restaurant and a manual labourer in a limestone quarry. At about this time, he began to read books of philosophy and theology, especially St John of the Cross. Under the Nazi occupation of his country, in 1942 he entered a banned seminary. He was ordained a priest on 1 November 1946 in Krakow, surprising many of his friends who expected him to pursue an acting career.

Karol Wojtyla's faith was a deeply intellectual one. His first doctorate, *The Doctrine of Faith According to Saint John of the Cross*, which must have given him much insight into the mystery and poetry of suffering, was unanimously approved in June 1948, but he was denied the degree because he could not afford to print the text of his dissertation. However, a revised text of his dissertation was approved in December of that year by the theological faculty of Jagiellonian University in Krakow, and Wojtyla was finally awarded the degree. His second doctorate, *An Evaluation of the Possibility of Constructing a Christian Ethics on the Basis of the System of Max Scheler*, was completed in 1954; however the faculty at Jagiellonian University was forbidden by the communist authorities from granting the degree. He finally obtained his second doctorate in philosophy in 1957 from the Catholic University of Lublin, Poland, where he assumed the Chair of Ethics in 1958.

As a recently ordained priest, he ministered to University of Kracow students at the Faculty of Medicine, a ministry he was devoted to for many years, even as Bishop and Archbishop.

By the age of 38 he was ordained Bishop, the youngest in Poland's history. As Archbishop he promoted, organised and defended the spiritual meetings which are still held at the Marian Sanctuary of Czestochowa for professional health workers, a revolution in their time, under the Polish Communist regime.

In 1967 he became the country's youngest Cardinal and at the age of 58, in 1978, he was elected Pontiff, the first non-Italian Pope for 450 years; not one expert had tipped him for the top job. A few hours after his election to the Papacy he amazed everyone by paying a hospital visit to Archbishop Andrew Maria Deskur. On that day Pope John Paul II declared that he wanted to: "…found my papacy above all on those that suffer and unite their prayers to suffering, passion and pains. Beloved brothers and sisters, I would like to entrust myself to your prayers… Just as the crucified Christ is powerful, so are you too powerful despite your physical state… your strength lies in your likeness to him. Use this force for the good of the Church, for your families, neighbours, countries and the entire humanity. Use it also for the good of the Pope's ministry, who in a certain sense is also very weak."[4]

Also on that special day he used the occasion of his first ever Papal audience to announce: "It is especially to the weakest, the sick, the poor, and the afflicted that we would like to open our hearts, in the initial moment of this pastoral ministry. Is it not you brothers and sisters, who indeed by your suffering share in the passion of the Saviour, and in a certain way do complete it? The unworthy successor of Peter who is set to pry into the unfathomable treasures of Christ, is in great need of your help, your sacrifice and prayer, and for this I humbly beseech you."[5]

In 1984 he published his great apostolic letter *Salvifici Doloris,* On the Christian Meaning of Suffering. The one to whom we put the question of suffering, says John Paul II, "...is himself suffering and wishes *to answer...*from the Cross, *from the heart of his own suffering...* Christ does not explain in the abstract the reasons for suffering but before all else he says: 'Follow me!' Come! Take part through your suffering in this work of saving the world... Gradually, *as the individual takes up his cross,* spiritually uniting himself to the Cross of Christ, the salvific meaning of suffering is revealed before him." The Pope, who in his lifetime had experienced the double pain of Nazi occupation and Communist oppression, knew that one of the most urgent tasks facing Christians is to reflect upon and help others to reflect upon the mystery of suffering – for when the mystery of suffering is misunderstood, the results are disastrous. As the Catechism of the Catholic Church states: "Illness and suffering have always been among the gravest problems confronted in human life. In illness, man experiences his powerlessness, his limitations, and his finitude. Every illness can make us glimpse death." (1500)

According to popular culture, suffering is meaningless, it is the great evil to be avoided by any means, whether it be abortion, euthanasia, infanticide, the isolation and even killing in the name of "mercy", of the sick, chronically ill, the elderly, the mentally ill, the disabled. At no point does Pope John Paul call suffering an evil in itself. Suffering, he says, has special value in the eyes of the Church.

Too often suffering is met with indifference, we pass by on the other side, the lonely mother, the distraught carer, the person in pain. Suffering is a call to action, to be a good Samaritan, to reach out to the whole world, in service, with love, mercy and compassion: "You sick people have an irreplaceable task: to be an inexhaustible source of peace and unity through your prayer and witness." (John Paul II in 1994, to a group of sick pilgrims.)[6]

In 1993, Pope John Paul II instituted the Annual World Day of the Sick. The event is held on 11 February each year, on the feast of Our Lady of Lourdes. In John Paul's message for that First Annual World Day of the Sick, he offered these words of comfort to suffering people around the world: "Your sufferings, accepted and borne with unshakeable faith, when joined to those of Christ take on extraordinary value for the life of the Church and the good of humanity." He also outlined how suffering can be transformed into something noble and good: "In the light of Christ's death and resurrection, illness no longer appears as an exclusively negative event," he said. "Rather, it is seen as... an opportunity to release love... to transform the whole of human civilisation into a civilisation of love. His final message for the Thirteenth Annual World Day of the Sick on 11 February 2005 was: "God has not forgotten you. Christ suffers with you. And by offering up your sufferings, you can collaborate with him in the redemption of the world."

Pope John Paul II was extremely popular worldwide, attracting the largest crowds in the history of the papacy (at times attracting crowds of over one million people in a single venue). He inspired millions to uphold human dignity and, in the eyes of many historians, helped bring about the collapse of communist rule in Europe. His messages, regardless of where he was in the world, focused on human rights, particularly the rights of young people.

Shot and almost killed in 1981, while leaning out of his vehicle, by Mehmet Ali Agca, a Turkish gunman, as he entered St Peters Square to address an audience, the Pope was hospitalised for months. Agca was caught and sentenced to life imprisonment. Two days after Christmas 1983, John Paul II visited him in prison. The two spoke privately for some time. John Paul II said, "What we talked about will have to remain a secret between him and me. I spoke to him as a brother whom I have pardoned and who has my complete trust." Agca was released on parole from a Turkish prison in January 2006.

In the early 1990s health problems began to take their toll. In 1992, the Holy Father had colon surgery, the next year he fell and dislocated a shoulder and suffered from arthritis of the knee. In 1994, he suffered a broken femur, in 1996 he had an appendectomy. His Parkinson's type disease also began to develop at about this time. He stopped walking in public in 2003 and stopped celebrating public liturgies in 2004.

TIME magazine named Pope John Paul II 'Man of the Year' in 1994, remarking upon his room: "as spare as a monk's. The room contains a single bed, two straight-backed upholstered chairs, a desk. There is a small carpet near the bed, but otherwise the parquet floor is bare. The walls too are unembellished except for a few souvenirs, mostly icons." He was, the magazine reported, a man of deep prayer: "Sometimes John Paul will prostrate himself before the altar. At other times he will sit or kneel with eyes closed, his forehead cradled in his left hand, his face contorted intensely, as if in pain. At this time, too, he brings to his God the prayer requests of others. His *prie-dieu*, at the front centre of the chapel, has a padded armrest. It lifts up, and underneath there is a small container for a couple of prayer books and a big stack of intentions, written on yellow sheets. Last month the stack was 200 sheets thick, and the one on the top had nine different names written on it, including that of a 17-year-old Italian boy with cancer, an Italian mother of three who was very sick and an American child."[7]

He knew intimately what it is to grieve, to be sick, to be disabled, to be rendered helpless, as he expressed in a 1997 address to health care workers: " Every day I try to be close to your sufferings. I can say this because I am familiar with the experience of a hospital bed. Precisely because of this, with greater insistence in my daily prayer I beseech God for you, asking him to give you strength and health... From a human point of view the situation of a sick person is difficult, painful and sometimes even humiliating. But it is precisely because of this that you are in a special way close to Christ, and in a certain sense share physically in his sacrifice. Try to remember this.[8]

Pope John Paul II maintained his commitment to the sick right to the end. In 1985 he founded the Pontifical Council for Pastoral Assistance to Health Care Work. Addressing that Council in January 2005, four months before his own death, he yet again emphasised the special role of the sick in the Church saying how: "the sick person can joyfully discover *the particular mission* entrusted to the sick in the Mystical Body of the Church: united with the suffering Christ, each one can cooperate in the salvation of humanity, making the most of his or her prayers with the offering up of one's suffering" (cf. Col 1:24).

In his Letter to the Elderly (1999), John Paul II beautifully summed up the joy of Christian hope and his own faith-filled response to suffering and death:

I find great peace in thinking of the time when the Lord will call me: from life to life! And so I often find myself saying, with no trace of melancholy, a prayer recited by priests after the celebration of the Eucharist: *In hora mortis meae voca me, et iube me venire ad te* – at the hour of my death, call me and bid me come to you. This is the prayer of Christian hope, which in no way detracts from the joy of the present, while entrusting the future to God's gracious and loving care.

Grant, O Lord of Life, that we may be ever vividly aware of this, and that we may savour every season of our lives as a gift filled with promise for the future.

Grant that we may lovingly accept your will, and place ourselves each day in your merciful hands.

And when the moment of our definitive "passage" comes, grant that we may face it with serenity, without regret for what we shall leave behind. For in meeting you, after having sought you for so long, we shall find once more every authentic good which we have known here on earth, in the company of all who have gone before us marked with the sign of faith and hope.

On 31 March 2005, the Pope developed a very high fever. Later that day Vatican sources announced that John Paul II had been given the Anointing of the Sick. During the final days of the Pope's life, the lights were kept burning through the night where he lay in the Papal apartment. Thousands of pilgrims filled St Peter's Square, holding vigil for two days. At about 3.30pm John Paul II spoke his final words, "Let me go to the house of the Father." He died at 9.37pm on Saturday, 2 April 2005, in his private apartments, just as the vigil of the Second Sunday of Easter, that is, Divine Mercy Sunday, was being commemorated.

In his last will and testament Pope John Paul II wrote:

> In the Name of the Holiest Trinity. Amen.
> "Keep watch, because you do not know which day when the Lord will come." – These words remind me of the final call, which will come the moment that the Lord will choose. I desire to follow him and desire that all that is part of my earthly life shall prepare me for this moment. I do not know when it will come, but, like all else, this moment too I place into the hands of the Mother of my Master: *Totus Tuus.*

Totus tuus ego sum, was always the Holy Father's motto – it means "I am completely in your hands". On the front page of every document he wrote, those words would be inscribed and on the top left of every page he would write the letters AMDG (initials for *Ad Majorem Dei Gloriam* – To the Greater Glory of God).

At his funeral, attended by Kings, Prime Ministers and Presidents, Cardinal Ratzinger – to emotional applause – pointed to Pope John Paul's studio window and said: "We can be sure that our beloved pope is standing today at the window of the Father's house, that he sees us and blesses us." He said John Paul was a "priest to the last" and that he had offered his life for God and his flock "especially amid the sufferings of his final months".

Beyond Normal Prayer

Dear brothers and sisters, proclaim and bear witness to the Gospel of life and hope with generous dedication. Proclaim that Christ is the comfort of all who are in distress or difficulty; he is the strength of those experiencing moments of fatigue and vulnerability; he is the support of those who work zealously to assure better living and health conditions for everyone.

The message of Pope John Paul II for the World Day of the Sick, 11 February 2001.

This is the prayer of the heart, not the prayer of the head. This is the prayer of being, not doing. This is the prayer of love unbound. This is the prayer of really entering into the mystery of the Trinity and becoming enwrapped by love.

This prayer is not about asking to be made well, not about asking for a cure or taking pain away. It is going beyond and within your experience to the uncreated energy of God. It is when you just have to be in the place of suffering. This is when you cling to God. This is the poverty of spirit that unleashes the power of the Holy Spirit into your life. This is the emptying of self that becomes the fullness of God. This is where letting go leads to a new beginning and welcoming, into the wonder and true reality of God with us. The finding of mercy becomes the finding of love unconditional, flowing ever-present, awesome, incredible, amazing in its breadth, height and depth. There is a breaking open of experience that enters into a new dimension of awareness of light, where you feel

God's presence, where you know God's peace truly beyond the horror of the present moment. It truly is the gift of peace not of this world, just as Jesus said.

It is that which enters into the places between the pain and make it possible to live within. It is that wonderful, beyond-words dimension of knowing God that lifts, sustains and brings hope and power and possibility into the seemingly impossible.

Words are truly not necessary, for God knows all. He loves all and reunites us with the truth that lies beyond and within all suffering; the pearl of great price, the light of man, the Word of God, the awesome Trinity, love indefinable and all-encompassing, flowing in Spirit, blessing each moment, touching our lives and through us radiating out into the whole world in a unity of being and wonder that can only be described as love.

Appendix 1

Prayers for the sick and suffering
(with kind permission of Linda Crowhurst)

Christ wants us all to say yes, to come to him, to find his hope and healing peace. In accepting him, in growing relationship, in aliveness of love, all things are possible and nothing is wasted.

Each moment's suffering can be a gift to help heal the universe, each tear can be a healing gift of love, and each joy-filled moment can bless the world.

So let us say "Yes" and receive gifts in abundance from the One who is love.

Litany to the heart of love

O heart of love, O mighty Trinity,
    pour out your grace upon us.

O heart of love, O mighty Trinity,
    grant our acceptance of your loving service.

O heart of love, O mighty Trinity,
    bless our lives.

O heart of love, O mighty Trinity,
    teach us the word of God.

O heart of love, O mighty Trinity,
    fill us with compassion.

O heart of love, O mighty Trinity,
    release our tears.

O heart of love, O mighty Trinity,
    free us from sin.

O heart of love, O mighty Trinity,
    help us to bear our burdens lightly.

O heart of love, O mighty Trinity,
    lead us to Mercy.

O heart of love, O mighty Trinity,
    unite us in the Trinity.

O heart of love, O mighty Trinity,
    bless us with miracles.

O heart of love, O mighty Trinity,
    transfigure us with your light.

O heart of love, O mighty Trinity,
    feed us with the perfect bread of heaven.

O heart of love, O mighty Trinity,
    bring us to life.

O heart of love, O mighty Trinity,
    be with us in our discipleship.

O heart of love, O mighty Trinity,
    guide us in prayer.

O heart of love, O mighty Trinity,
    open our hearts to accept your love.

O heart of love, O mighty Trinity,
    let us give glory to God forevermore.

O heart of love, O mighty Trinity,
    surround..................................(*individual petition/s*) with your love.

followed by

O heart of love, most holy Trinity,
    surround us with your love. Amen.

Linda Crowhurst

In lifting others up to the Love of God all things are possible – all love is given back.

Prayer then is two-way – we, too, are blessed by our compassion and love for others. We, too, are held in his grace in that connection with divine love.

In praying we are touched by his love. In holding others in his love we, too, are held. There is such love then and intimacy in prayer – which truly is relationship with God.

No wonder we are asked to 'pray without ceasing'!

A prayer of trust

Lord,
in all things
I trust in you.

When fear
overwhelms me
I turn to you.

When doubt
assails me
I turn to you.

When peace
is lost
I turn to you.

When anxieties
mob me
I turn to you.

When pain
oppresses me
I turn to you.

When worries
betray me
I turn to you.

Lord,
in all things
I am held by You. Amen

Linda Crowhurst

Hold us up prayer

We hold ourselves up to you, Lord:
in you we are held.
We open our hearts to you, Lord:
in you our hearts are opened up.
We ask for your help, Lord:
in you we are helped.
We ask for your healing power, Lord:
in you we are healed.
We ask for your forgiveness, Lord:
in you we are forgiven.
We ask to serve you, Lord:
in you we serve.
We lift each hurting soul up to you, Lord:
in you they are lifted up.

Linda Crowhurst

Mary stood at the foot of the cross and suffered in silence with Christ – united in love, the pain must have been immense, unbearable – to see her beloved one suffer, to feel helpless, but to still stay by him.

There is much power in offering up such pain as this for the healing of the world. If we can remember that in the heart of our own grief, we can still give a gift of love; nothing is wasted and love returns multiplied. Mary's love for her Son brings her the grace of God and because she suffered so closely with her Son, how closely she can empathise with us in our pain, especially when it arises from a feeling of helplessness and abandonment.

Because Mary is so close and has known the infinite suffering of Christ, he will always hear our prayers when we ask Mary to intercede. Because she suffered so, this shared suffering brings an even greater gift of love and hope. I dedicate this prayer especially to all people who care for someone in pain.

Mary weeping at the Cross:

may your tears heal the earth
may your tears touch our hearts
may your tears cleanse our soul

may your grief heal our grief
may your grief touch our emptiness
may your grief speak for us

may your love heal our fear
may your love touch our pain
may your love bless our lives

may your hope heal our hearts
may your hope touch our souls
may your hope guide us on
                    to your Son.

Come into the hurting places

These words came from my own need to be healed on every level: mind, body, emotion and spirit. The pain and illness I experience touches every level, and so I find the healing that is needed must be on all levels too.

I felt like I was crying out for healing. If only God would come into all of me, not only the nice OK parts or the places I have worked on and feel good about, but all the deepest hidden hurts as well, even the ones I cannot express or even remember – all need his perfect love to embrace them – to be filled with the fullness of God so that transformation might occur.

This prayer is a cry of the heart, for love to come and accept all of me.

Come into the hurting places if you will

Come gently into the hurting places of my body:
caress them gently if you will,
tenderly heal them if you will.

Come gently now into the hurting places of
    my heart:
release the many unshed tears if you will,
fill my vulnerability with your strength if you will.

Come gently now into the hurting places of
    my mind:
touch each painful moment with love
    if you will,
lift my thoughts to higher places if you will.

Come gently now into the hurting places of
    my soul:
let your light pour into me if you will,
give me the gifts of your spirit if you will.

Come into the hurting places if you will,
and make me whole.

Linda Crowhurst

Thanking and praising are wonderful ways to reach up to the glory and wonder of God – they help us to see things in a different light – to feel all possibilities rather than limitation – they help us see clearly and find hope again. We are then lifted into the wonderful presence of God where all things are possible and all healing is already complete. It is a way of saying 'Yes' to love and light and beauty – to seeing the truth and experiencing the wonder of God.

Lord, for the opportunity to come together –
    we thank you.
Lord, for space to hear you – we thank you.
Lord, for each other – we thank you.
Lord, for the gift of love – we thank you.
Lord, for the grace to open up – we thank you.
Lord, for wisdom and discernment – we
    thank you.
Lord, for the grace of forgiveness – we thank you.
Lord, for this time of sharing – we thank you.
Amen.

Sometimes we just need to be held – to know that in our anxiety and fear God will hold us and that his love is tender and full of compassion.

Words are not always needed – a touch can convey everything, can bless and heal and keep us safe.

When love touches us we feel better.

Amen

Let us say "Yes" to you.
Let us open our hearts
and say a resounding "Yes" of love,
A "Yes" that opens us instantly
to the abundance of heaven.
Let us say "Yes" to you
with all the heavenly hosts.

Let us sing your glorious name
in absolute abandon,
and be filled again and again
with the joy of the angels
who ever live in your presence
and see your most beautiful face.
Let us dare to say "Yes" to you
then follow in all confidence
the path that lies open –
the path that leads straight to you.
Let us sing a resounding "Yes" of love
and be happy forever more.

Linda Crowhurst

What does it mean to say "Yes" to God? It means that you cannot be stuck; that all things become possible – healing, hope, transformation, miracles – because "Yes" means opening up our hearts and accepting love right in. It means you are not alone – there is One who can and will help – it means trust and faith become central in your life, it means living in relationship with God. It means peace is possible whatever the situation and that really there is no need to fear because he is with you and will come to live in you – his promise, if only we can open our hearts and say "Yes" to his love.

Let us hope in miracles.
Let us trust in miracles.
Let us believe in the miracle
of your love.

God hears every prayer and every second of our life is precious to him. Sometimes when things are difficult it is hard to keep trusting or believing that he is hearing our cry; this is when faith is needed.

We can only hope and pray that he will keep us safe and bring us through. We cannot always remember his goodness and love and so sometimes we need to pray and ask for help to remember they are there.

Sometimes we cannot see how healing will happen, sometimes it is not always in the way that we hope for, but always we must trust that if we give it to God there will be healing, however it manifests and whenever it manifests.

Sometimes we need to let go of trying to control the outcomes. This is the hardest thing!

ENDNOTES

1   Frossard, A. *Non Abbiate Paura* (Rusconi, 4th edition, July 1983), p.12.
2   ibid.
3   Poltawska, W. 'Il Ruolo della Famiglia nello Svillupo della Personalità' in *Dolentium Hominum*, no. 16 (1-1991), p.86.
4   Cf. John Paul II, Address to the Sick and Health Care Workers, on occasion of his first visit to "Gemelli" General Hospital, 18 October 1978, in *L'Osservatore Romano* (Italian Edit.), *Salvifici Doloris* 19 October 1978, pp.1-2.
5   Cf. John Paul II, the first Audience held by him in the Sistine Chapel, on *Salvifici Doloris*, 18 October 1978, in *l'Osservatore Romano* (Italian edit.), 19 October 1978, p.1.
6   John Paul II, Greeting of the Holy Father to the group of the sick people gathered in the central nave of the Shrine of Loreto, 10 December 1994, in *Dolentium Hominum*, n. 29/1995, p.18.
7   Elson, J. (1994) 'Man of the Year John Paul II', TIME Magazine, 26 December 1994, vol 11, No. 26.
8   Cf. John Paul II, the Address to all Health Care Workers in occasion of the visit and blessing of the new heart surgery clinic of "John Paul II Hospital" in Krakow, June 9, 1997, in *Dolentium Hominum* n. 36/1997, p.17.